ABOUT THIS BOOK

The illustrations in the book were painted in Acryla Gouache on Cold Press illustration board, and then scanned and assembled in a digital collage. This book was edited by Nikki Garcia and designed by Véronique Lefèvre Sweet. The production was supervised by Erika Schwartz, and the production editor was Jen Graham. The text was set in Goudy Old Style Bold, and the display type is Naive Inline Shadow Bold.

Photo credits: Page 39, clockwise from top left: © George Rinhart/Corbis; Smithsonian National Air and Space Museum (NASM 92-13721); Smithsonian National Air and Space Museum (NASM 99-15416); Smithsonian National Air and Space Museum (NASM 86-6177). Page 41: © neftali/Shutterstock.com.
Background image and texture inside ornaments on endpapers and pages 2, 5, 7, 8, 11, 15, 16, 19, 20, 23, 26, 29, 30, 33, 34, 36, 38, and 41 © VolodymyrSanych/Shutterstock.com and somchaiP/Shutterstock.com.
Ornaments on pages 2, 5, 7, 8, 11, 12, 15, 16, 19, 20, 23, 25, 26, 29, 30,w33, 34, 36, 38, 40, and 41 © LukyToky/Shutterstock.com.

Little, Brown and Company • Hachette Book Group • 1290 Avenue of the Americas, New York, NY 10104 • Visit us at LBYR.com

First Edition: December 2020

Little, Brown and Company is a division of Hachette Book Group, Inc.
The Little, Brown name and logo are trademarks of Hachette Book Group, Inc.

The publisher is not responsible for websites (or their content) that are not owned by the publisher.

Library of Congress Cataloging-in-Publication Data
Names: Parsons, Karyn, 1968– author. | Christie, R. Gregory, 1971– illustrator.
Title: Flying free : how Bessie Coleman's dreams took flight / by Karyn Parsons ; illustrated by R. Gregory Christie.
Other titles: How Bessie Coleman's dreams took flight
Description: New York : Little, Brown and Company, [2020] | Series: A sweet blackberry book | Includes bibliographical references. | Audience: Ages 4–8 | Summary: "The story of Bessie Coleman, the first African American woman to earn her pilot's license"— Provided by publisher.
Identifiers: LCCN 2019051389 | ISBN 9780316457194 (hardcover) | ISBN 9780316457217 (ebook) | ISBN 9780316457187 (ebook other)
Subjects: LCSH: Coleman, Bessie, 1896–1926—Juvenile literature. | African American women air pilots—Biography—Juvenile literature. | Air pilots—United States—Biography—Juvenile literature.
Classification: LCC TL540.C546 P37 2020 | DDC 629.13092 [B]—dc23
LC record available at https://lccn.loc.gov/2019051389

ISBN: 978-0-316-45719-4 (hardcover)

PRINTED IN CHINA

APS

10 9 8 7 6 5 4 3 2 1

FLYING FREE
HOW BESSIE COLEMAN'S DREAMS TOOK FLIGHT

By **KARYN PARSONS**

Illustrated by **R. GREGORY CHRISTIE**

Little, Brown and Company

New York Boston

Bessie Coleman was born
A spirited little girl
Whose sense of adventure
Would light the whole world.

In the morning, she'd rise
And breathe the fresh air.
Marvel at the small flocks of birds
Flying there.

Bessie loved reading.
Loved math and science, too.
As she excelled in her studies,
Her confidence grew.

But each end of summer,
When harvest came around,
Her family got to picking cotton
And the schools would close down.

Hands sore from that picking,
Bessie wiped her small brow
And dreamed she'd find greatness.
She just didn't know how.

Black bird. Black girl.

Shine bright for the whole world.

Show your spark. Show your twirl.

Let those beautiful wings unfurl!

One day, Bessie's teacher
Told them of how
A woman had become a pilot!
A huge breakthrough! Wow!

Harriet Quimby
Was the brave woman's name,
And being the first
Had brought her new fame.

While the kids all snickered
And shook their heads,
Bessie thought hard
About what her teacher had said.

Bessie kept working the fields.
Got a job cleaning clothes.
Saved up her money
For when opportunity arose.

Bessie loved Waxahachie.
Loved her family even more.
But she longed to go
Where her spirit could soar.

One day, her brother wrote,
"Why don't you come?
Join me in Chicago!
We'll have loads of fun!"

Very soon she found work.
Not one job, but two!
Serving up chili
And doing nails, too.

At the salon one day,
Her brother strolled in,
Charming all with his war tales
That he told with a grin.

The French fliers, he said,
Were heroic and true,
But what impressed him the most
Were the women who flew.

"To fly!" said Bessie.
"I'd love to! I would!"
"Ha!" laughed her brother.
"There's no way that you could!

"You live in America,
Are black and female.
You'd have a better chance
If you had a tail!"

Bessie said, "Oh yeah?
You just wait and see!
There'll be a black female pilot.
And it will be ME!"

Black bird. Black girl.
Shine bright for the whole world.
Show your spark. Show your twirl.
Let those beautiful wings unfurl!

They all told her, "No!
We won't teach you to fly!
You're a girl! The wrong color!"
But she still had to try.

Then a friend told her,
"I think you'd have a chance
If you didn't stay here
But instead went to France.

"I'll pay for your trip!
Yes! Give it a go!
When you come home a pilot,
The whole country will know!"

"*Je m'appelle Bessie!*"
She'd soon made a date
To travel to FRANCE.
She could hardly wait!

Sometimes it was hard
Being so far from home.
Sometimes she felt sad
And terribly alone.

The work was quite hard,
But she enjoyed her training.
With so much to do, there was
No time for complaining.

This was her calling!
The sky was for her.
There it didn't matter
What color you were.

X.
Paris,
France

Black bird. Black girl.
Shine bright for the whole world.
Show your spark. Show your twirl.
Let those beautiful wings unfurl!

When it was finally time
To get her license to fly,
Bessie passed all the tests
On the *very first try!!!*

There it was, in her hand,
Her PILOT'S LICENSE!
She couldn't wait to show it
To her family and friends!

Upon her return,
Triumphant and proud,
Bessie was greeted
By a loud, cheering crowd.

Her picture made news.
There it was, FRONT PAGE!
"1ST BLACK FEMALE PILOT!"
She was all the rage!

The best way, she thought,
To show her new skills
Was to hold flying shows,
Full of daring thrills.

The crowds loved it all.
Her stunts, how she dressed.
An enchanting daredevil!
They nicknamed her Queen Bess!

She would fight racism
At her air shows, too.
Would tell the officials
To integrate the venue.

"I won't do the show
If you segregate!
Black folks and white
Must come in the same gate!"

Bessie traveled the country.
Spoke to young and to old,
Inspiring all races
With the stories she told.

All these years later
Brave Bessie still inspires.
Many people of color
Have since become fliers.

Above the land. Above the sea.
Where they all said she shouldn't be.
Bessie said, "Watch!" She said, "You'll see!"
And followed her dream, flying free.

TRAILBLAZING WOMEN IN FLIGHT

✦ October 7, 1908: Edith Berg becomes the first American woman to fly as an airplane passenger.

✦ October 22, 1909: Raymonde de Laroche (born Elise Raymonde Deroche) is the first woman to pilot a solo flight in an airplane.

✦ March 8, 1910: Raymonde de Laroche becomes the first woman to earn a pilot's license.

✦ 1910: Hilda Hewlett becomes the first British female pilot and the first woman to cofound a flight school.

✦ May 1911: Hélène Dutrieu is the first woman to win an air race.

✦ August 1, 1911: Harriet Quimby becomes the first American woman to earn a pilot's license.

✦ April 16, 1912: Harriet Quimby is the first woman to fly across the English Channel.

✦ June 21, 1913: Georgia "Tiny" Broadwick is the first woman to parachute from an airplane.

✦ 1913: Ruth Law is the first woman to fly at night.

✦ 1915: French native Marie Marvingt is the first woman to fly in combat, during World War I.

✦ June 15, 1921: Bessie Coleman becomes the first African American to earn a pilot's license.

✦ 1929: Florence Lowe "Pancho" Barnes becomes the first female stunt pilot in Hollywood.

✦ May 20–21, 1932: Amelia Earhart is the first woman to fly solo across the Atlantic Ocean.

✦ 1938: Willa Brown is the first African American woman to earn her pilot's license in the United States.

✦ May 18, 1953: Jackie Cochran becomes the first woman to break the sound barrier.

✦ April 17, 1964: Geraldine "Jerrie" Mock is the first woman to fly around the world.

✦ March 2, 1973: Women begin aviation training for the US Navy.

✦ June 6, 1976: Emily Howell Warner becomes the first female airline captain in the United States.

✦ 1978: Jill Brown-Hiltz becomes the first African American woman to fly for a major commercial airline in the United States.

✦ 1979: Marcella Ng becomes the first African American to earn her aviator wings in the US military.

✦ 1990: Patrice Washington becomes the first black female pilot to fly for UPS.

✦ 1993: Matice Wright becomes the first African American female flight officer in the US Navy.

✦ August 8, 1997: Jennifer Murray is the first woman to fly around the world in a helicopter.

✦ November 1998: Melissa "M'Lis" Ward becomes the first African American woman to captain for United Airlines, a major US commercial airline.

✦ 2003: Vernice Armour is recognized by the Department of Defense as America's first African American female combat pilot.

✦ February 12, 2009: The first all–African American female flight crew flies a commercial plane in the United States.

✦ 2009: Kimberly Anyadike becomes the youngest African American woman to pilot a plane solo across the United States, at fifteen years old.

Bessie Coleman, the first black female pilot in the world, on January 24, 1923.

Bessie standing on the wheel of her plane, which she named Jennie, in 1924.

The Curtiss JN-4 is the type of aircraft that Bessie flew.

The Fédération Aéronautique Internationale awarded Bessie Coleman her pilot's license in 1921.

AUTHOR'S NOTE

I WAS WELL INTO ADULTHOOD WHEN I FIRST HEARD OF BESSIE COLEMAN. I was cast in a play entitled *Bird Girl* by Anne Harris, in the role of Bessie, a female aviator who comes to the play's protagonist in her dreams. Bessie was a guide of sorts. This introduction would lead to more curiosity about her, extending far beyond my brief portrayal of her.

When I first started Sweet Blackberry, the mission of the organization was to bring little-known stories of African American achievement to children. It still is, but at that time, we were only producing short, animated films—inspiring and empowering stories of men and women who overcame incredible obstacles and went on to do great things.

Bessie was an obvious choice.

Shortly after I decided to include her story in the Sweet Blackberry series, I began discovering mini biographies and other books about Bessie. Not many, but more than the other "little-known" subjects I had lined up to create films around. Did Bessie really fit into the unsung-hero mold? I wasn't sure. I decided that, as much as I loved Bessie, we wouldn't create a film about her life after all. So I went on to write about and produce other subjects and their stories.

But Bessie never left me.

I found myself bringing her up from time to time whenever I discussed Sweet Blackberry's mission and was surprised that I was often met with "Oh, yes, I know Bessie Smith."

I'd have to correct the person.

"No, not the singer. Bessie *Coleman*, the aviator."

I was beginning to see that most folks had no idea about the incredible, groundbreaking "Queen Bess."

Eventually, I determined that not enough people knew who she was. And while I thought I had a good sense of who she was, I really didn't, either.

Instead, I discovered a person I had a hard time relating to. While I may have made choices that to some seem bold, I have spent most of my life staying within the boundaries drawn around me. I grew up in the 1970s and 80s, when black people and women were allowed to vote, to freely obtain an education, to travel where they wanted when they wanted. In the United States there were few binds on my actions—and nothing close to the limitations imposed on Bessie in the 1920s.

As I read Bessie's story, I found myself often stopping to survey the photo of her in her pilot's cap and jacket, smiling bright. Studying her face for any clues of her bravery. Was there a way to tell just by looking at her that she was so clever? So unstoppable?

Bessie recognized that she was so much more than the world around her would have her believe. She didn't need anyone to tell her who she was or what she was capable of. *She* knew.

I hung Bessie's picture above my desk and kept it there long after I'd finished writing her story. She provided immeasurable inspiration to me and was my reminder that *I* knew what I was capable of. Whenever I had doubts, I turned to Bessie.

Bessie's determination inspired generations of men, women, and children. I hope that this book will introduce many more young, curious minds to this revolutionary woman and that, by witnessing her boldness and dedication, they will recognize what they, too, are capable of.

ARTIST'S NOTE

IT'S TOO OFTEN THAT HISTORICAL FEATS AND FIGURES LOSE THEIR IMPACT WITH THE PASSAGE OF TIME. Many of your great-grandparents' heroes may have slipped out of context completely in our modern society. So I feel elated when projects such as *Flying Free: How Bessie Coleman's Dreams Took Flight* are offered to me to illustrate.

This nonprofit endeavor from Sweet Blackberry first started as an animated historical DVD. An accomplishment that was previously a footnote in our history classes moves beyond a paragraph into a tangible picture book. And I hope it will help you balance your bookshelves.

Sweet Blackberry helps Bessie Coleman historically stand strong with Amelia Earhart and Harriet Quimby. But Bessie stands apart for me because she knew the balance between spirit-breaking, small-town obscurity and worldwide fame. As you study her life, you see that she was not only an inspiration but also a straight-shooting activist. And even through all the scrutiny and racism, Bessie Coleman remained headstrong and learned to fly in the figurative and literal sense.

Bessie grew up in a time when it was a societal norm for women to have nowhere near the same rights as men. Bessie's achievements go beyond the spectacular. She came from some of Texas's poorest regions with her Native and African American roots. Distinctions between wealth, class, gender, and race were strongly defined during these times. For example, a woman was at risk of arrest for publicly wearing anything too casual, because in Bessie's youth, modesty in the form of long skirts and corsets was a typical way life. A great stress was placed on how a woman behaved during these times, and I thought about these factors as I visually recounted her biography.

Bessie's story spoke to me because it captured the highs and lows of her experiences in a child-friendly way. It told of her time in Paris, her excitement of being there along with the loneliness and hard work it took to stay and persevere. *Flying Free* shows her in a human light, as she grew from an aspiring pilot with doubts and restrictions into a first-ever pilot experiencing fame and joy.

My illustrations were inspired by photographs from Bessie's era, and I researched old photos of other families from that region

A Black Heritage stamp showing Bessie Coleman, circa 1995.

of Texas as well as the overall fashion of the day. I'm so honored to put my paint, brushes, and interpretation to the ways Bessie redefined what it was to be accepted. She broke boundaries in our society and in her field of aviation. It's a story that needs to be celebrated. My hope for readers is that the inspiring history found within the words will open up visual ideas and colors as expansive as Bessie's sky.